KAISER WILHELM II

A Life From Beginning to End

Copyright © 2018 by Hourly History.

Table of Contents

Introduction

Kaiser Wilhelm II reigned during the World War I era, and some would say he is responsible for the breakout of that war altogether. He served as the last German emperor and the king of Prussia, and it was the changes he made to German foreign policies that some say led to the start of the First World War.

Wilhelm's background was mixed. He was born of parents who were from Prussia and England. As he grew up, he would identify with the German and Prussian side of the family more. Later, he would go as far as speaking down on the British, disregarding the fact that his own heritage went back to England on one side of his family.

Wilhelm was quite intelligent, but he was also arrogant and self-serving. He had a hot temper and could be very impulsive. In his time as Kaiser, Wilhelm managed to offend many of his peers and much of society. He damaged his reputation over and over, just by being himself and showing off his high-strung personality. While others before him had worked very hard to try to stabilize Europe and keep peace within the continental borders, Wilhelm seemed to work tirelessly at stirring up conflict with many of Germany's neighbors, as well as with countries in other parts of the world. His scant efforts at diplomacy were often overshadowed by his pompous attitude about Germany and what he felt his country was entitled to. He often disregarded public opinion, seeing it as less important than his own opinion.

Wilhelm's time spent leading Germany was riddled with alienation, leading to his own self-destruction and the ruin of the German Empire as it was once known. In 1918, 30 years after he had taken over as the German emperor from his father, Wilhelm II had lost all support from the army. He abdicated from his position as the leader of the German Empire and Prussia and spent the rest of his life in exile in the Netherlands.

The reign of Kaiser Wilhelm II may seem to be full of blunders. But the world's history was shaped heavily by this man's political moves, however disliked he may have been. He spent a lot of time offending others and not by accident. He wasn't discreet when talking about people; in fact, the term "behind the back" didn't apply to Wilhelm. Others always knew what he thought of them because he was forthright in his opinions and insults. He often spoke down to people or made fun of them right to their faces. His life, to some degree, may not have been one to call well-lived, but it has had an immense impact on how the world has turned out to be in present day.

Chapter One

Born with a Disability

"Germany must have her place in the sun."

—Kaiser Wilhelm II

Born under the name Friedrich Wilhelm Viktor Albert von Hohenzollern, Kaiser Wilhelm II would go down in history as an often frowned upon leader in the World War I time period.

Wilhelm was born on January 27, 1859. His father, Prince Frederick Wilhelm, was from Prussia while his mother, Princess Victoria, was from England. While Wilhelm's ties to the English royal family did play a role in some of the political moves he would make during his reign as the German emperor, those ties wouldn't be strong enough to solidify any kind of soft spot in Wilhelm's heart for Britain. He would still maneuver things politically to end up sparking World War I where the German Empire and Great Britain were on opposite sides of the fight.

Wilhelm was born as second in line to rule Prussia as his great-uncle Frederick William IV was the king of Prussia at the time of his birth. Later, Wilhelm would also become next in line to be the German emperor. There was no formal political German Empire when Wilhelm was born however—the so-called Second Reich would not be founded until 1871 when Germany was unified.

One key event in Wilhelm's early life that helped shape him into the man he became later in life was his birth, which was very traumatic for both Wilhelm and his mother. The doctor who was attempting to deliver Wilhelm was having a difficult time getting the baby boy out of the birth canal. The complications of his delivery resulted in a left arm that was much smaller than his other arm and was also quite useless for many everyday tasks. In his adult years, Wilhelm became quite good at hiding his disability. He was especially good at covering it up in portraits. He would pose his arm to make it look as if it was useful in some way, use props that would make the arm look longer, or distract the viewer from seeing that his left arm was withered and shorter than the right arm. Many scholars think that the disability Wilhelm was born with stunted his emotional growth and contributed to him making reckless decisions throughout his reign as Kaiser and king.

From very early on, Wilhelm had a volatile temper and would often act out of anger. When he was only four years old, he was taken to England to attend his uncle's royal wedding. His outfit for the wedding was completed with a tiny toy dirk; a dirk was a small dagger carried by Scotsmen of the time. Wilhelm got a bit antsy during the wedding ceremony, and his uncle who was watching over him tried to get the boy to be still. But Wilhelm wasn't having any of it. He pulled his dirk and pointed it at his uncle, threatening him to stay away. His uncle attempted to physically restrain the child, so Wilhelm bit his uncle on the leg.

Wilhelm was the first-born grandchild to Queen Victoria of England. She and her grandson had a good relationship and were quite fond of each other in his early years. She missed all the ruckus with the leg biting incident and saw her grandson as a good little boy with a sweet disposition.

Princess Victoria, the queen's daughter, on the other hand, worried a lot about Wilhelm when he was growing up. She became almost obsessive about her son's arm and felt a lot of guilt that he had to live with the disability. She thought she was responsible for the complications that arose during childbirth, and she worried about him being hindered in life because of his resulting disability. It haunted Princess Victoria's thoughts that an heir to the throne might not be capable of riding as he should. So, she made it a mission: Wilhelm was going to learn to ride a horse, no matter what it took.

At about eight years old, Wilhelm began taking lessons to learn how to ride. It was almost torturous for the young boy. He would sit on the back of the horse with tears streaming down his face. He fell off time after time after time. Made worse by his useless arm, his balance was the biggest issue. It took several weeks of continuous lessons, but in the end Wilhelm was capable of doing it; he would ride a horse as the Prussian king, disability or not.

When Wilhelm was 12 years old, in 1871, the German Empire was formally and politically formed as its own national entity. The Empire was to be led by the Prussian king, and this occurrence boosted Wilhelm's enthusiasm for Prussian and German nationalistic views. Wilhelm was already second in line to be the king of Prussia, and the unification of Germany meant that he would also be second in line to be the German emperor.

In the meantime, Wilhelm had to finish his education. He was tutored as a young boy, but in his teenage years Wilhelm went to Friedrichsgymnasium in Kassel. He was a smart boy and did well in school. He graduated when he was 18 years old, and his grandmother Queen Victoria gave him a special gift, the Order of the Garter, which is one of the most prestigious orders of chivalry in Great Britain.

After his time spent in Kassel, Wilhelm went on to finish his education at the University of Bonn. He attended this college for four terms, studying law and politics. As with all of his other studies, Wilhelm performed well at university. The exclusive Corps Borussia Bonn made Wilhelm a member, of course. The group was the corps of the House of Hohenzollern, the royal dynasty and noble family of which Wilhelm as part.

Even though Wilhelm was born of both German and British descent, he gravitated more toward the nationalistic views of his father's side of the family. He was raised around the Prussian military groups and had been exposed to militant ideals from a very early age. Princess Victoria tried hard to teach her son about British liberalism. But Prussia was all about strong, manly military ideals, and Wilhelm believed in that way of life more and more the older he grew, following in the footsteps of his grandfather, Wilhelm I.

Chapter Two

Groomed for the Throne

"Woe and death to all who resist my will."

—Kaiser Wilhelm II

His grandfather watched as Wilhelm grew up and started turning into the man he wanted to see as an heir to the Prussian throne. Once Wilhelm turned 21, his grandfather thought it was time for him to start his military service. This phase was very important for anyone who was going to be ascending to the throne later on. Wilhelm was given the position of lieutenant and was assigned to the First Regiment of Foot Guards out of Potsdam, the place of his birth.

Wilhelm thrived in the military. This was the type of life he was meant to live. He got to be in an environment where he was surrounded by all of the things in which he believed so strongly and by people who believed in those same ideals. He said of his time in the military, "I really found my family, my friends, my interests—everything of which I had up to that time had to do without." Wilhelm had grown up speaking appropriately and politely, but while in the military, he really found his voice and started carrying himself with the esteem he deemed right for a military officer. He spoke with authority and never appeared to be less than confident in anything he said or did.

The further Wilhelm advanced in his military service, the more distant he became from his parents. Wilhelm thought that both of his parents were guilty of supporting the British liberalism above the Prussian and German Empire. Wilhelm had been tutored in his youth by a man named Georg Hinzpeter. Hinzpeter had very autocratic views and had laid the groundwork for Wilhelm's beliefs in the Prussian way of life. He had a very strong influence on what Wilhelm grew up to support.

In 1880, Wilhelm met his wife-to-be, Augusta Victoria of Schleswig-Holstein, known as "Dona." Wilhelm had previously fallen in love with one of his first cousins, Princess Elisabeth of Hesse-Darmstadt. He tried to get her to marry him, but Elisabeth refused his attempts at a proposal. She ended up marrying into the Russian imperial family instead. But Dona, on the other hand, accepted Wilhelm's marriage proposal, and the two became engaged. Dona and Wilhelm would be married for 40 years. Starting in 1882, during one decade of their marriage the couple had seven children together, six boys and one girl.

Following Wilhelm and Dona's wedding, Otto von Bismarck, a conservative Prussian statesman, started advocating to give Wilhelm privileges that had not been afforded to his father, the crown prince. Bismarck had plans for young Wilhelm and wanted to use him as a pawn to boost his own political standing. With Wilhelm as his weapon against the boy's parents, he could gain power himself.

In 1884, Bismarck started working on getting Wilhelm sent on different trips; he wanted him sent on diplomatic operations to countries where he had political interests. Prince Wilhelm's first trip of this kind was to St. Petersburg. He was to be in attendance at the coming of age ceremony for 16-year-old Tsarevich Nicholas in the court of Tsar Alexander III of Russia. Unfortunately, Wilhelm's behavior and attitude did not impress the Tsar.

In 1886, Wilhelm's grandfather took him on another diplomatic trip. They went to visit with the Austrian-Hungarian emperor, Franz Joseph. That trip went better thanks to the overseeing and influence of his grandfather, Kaiser Wilhelm I. Bismarck's son, Herbert von Bismarck, also started shaping Wilhelm that year. He spent two times a week putting the prince through Foreign Ministry training.

Bismarck spent these few years trying to get Wilhelm ready for the throne. He worked hard to create a rift between Wilhelm and his parents, but the rift would end up being between more than just he and his parents—it would eventually extend and cause a break between Wilhelm and Bismarck himself too. Bismarck was unknowingly supporting a prince who would turn out to be a leader but who would dismiss the chancellor from his position once he was in power.

As time went on, Wilhelm was influenced more and more to see England in a less than flattering light. He was denied the right to represent Germany at his grandmother's, Queen Victoria's, Golden Jubilee celebration in London in 1887. In the following year, Wilhelm would take over the throne from his father. The wedge in his mind separating him from his British ancestry was growing larger and larger.

In March of 1888, Wilhelm's father became Kaiser Frederick III of Germany. Wilhelm I had died on March 9, leaving Prussia and the German Empire with no leader. But Frederick's reign was short-lived. Kaiser Frederick III died after only a few months in power. He succumbed to throat cancer, which left the throne open to Wilhelm at the young age of 29.

Chapter Three

The Year of the Three Emperors

"Called to the throne of my fathers, I have taken over the government."

—Kaiser Wilhelm II

On June 15, 1888, only about three months after his father had been made the German emperor, Wilhelm ascended to the throne. He took over as the German Kaiser and the king of Prussia. His reign would last for 30 years and would change the world forever.

Conflict within his administration flared up quickly, especially with Otto von Bismarck. Wilhelm had maintained a good relationship with the statesman when he was younger, but by the time he took over the throne, he didn't agree with Bismarck's ideals of a peaceful foreign policy. Wilhelm was focused on Germany's place in the sun; he wanted more for Germany and believed the way to get that was to start forcefully extending their borders.

Wilhelm's grandfather had worked with Bismarck for a long time and had trusted him to take care of the day-to-day dealings of foreign policy. That was very different from Wilhelm's view on his position as emperor. He was not just reigning over the region, he would rule the land. That mindset would drive Wilhelm and Bismarck further and further apart.

Wilhelm may have been able to feel that Bismarck thought he was weak in a way. Bismarck had already shown some of what he thought of Wilhelm a few years back when he wanted to send him on all of those diplomatic missions. His intentions then had been to groom the young heir to the throne so that he could use him as a tool to gain more power and a better standing with Wilhelm's parents. Bismarck's thoughts of Wilhelm didn't change with his ascension to the throne. Bismarck saw him as someone he could dominate and sway to do what he wanted him to do. There were a lot of conflicts between the two men, and their relationship eventually became damaged beyond repair.

The final straw for Wilhelm came when Bismarck made an attempt to roll out an anti-socialist policy across the region. That move was more than Wilhelm was able to tolerate. In meetings with the administration, Wilhelm would make sure to interrupt Bismarck to show his disgust for Bismarck's foreign policy. At this point, Wilhelm started taking a lot of interest in social matters. One of those matters was the treatment of mine staffs. Wilhelm wanted to put laws into formality that would protect these workers and give them better lives. The Kaiser tried to push a proclamation through Council that would protect mine workers, but Bismarck declined to sign it. He opposed Wilhelm every chance he got because he felt unappreciated and devalued by the leader he had thought to be so easily dominated before.

The tension between these two men came to a head when Bismarck started looking for a new majority in Parliament. He had once held the majority with the *Kartell*. Now, without a majority, Bismarck wouldn't be able to push through any of the policies he supported. The *Kartell* had previously been voted out because of the anti-socialist bill Bismarck had tried rolling out earlier. There were two parties left that were in majority power: the Conservative Party and the Catholic Centre Party. Bismarck decided to try to gain the support of the Centre Party to make that his majority. He planned a meeting with Ludwig Windthorst who was the Centre Party's leader. In any state with Parliament, the members are permitted and expected to work with others and form coalitions. But when Wilhelm found out about the meeting, he was extremely angry. He didn't care that this was the norm for any parliamentary state. He felt that if Bismarck was going to meet with the head of one of the majority parties, the Kaiser should have been notified.

Wilhelm went to Bismarck's home in a fit of anger. The two had a heated argument, and Wilhelm schooled Bismarck on the rules of imperial authority. The conflict ended when Wilhelm left by storming out of the estate leaving Bismarck with no way to find an advantage. Bismarck had always been able to find ways to use events to his advantage, especially when it came to Wilhelm. This time, however, Wilhelm was demanding that Bismarck resign. Feeling forced by his leader, Bismarck wrote a lengthy and disgusted resignation letter to submit to Wilhelm. He wrote about his feelings toward Wilhelm's foreign policies and his stance on the ruling with the throne. After Bismarck died, the letter was published for the public to see.

Bismarck had done work with social security legislature in the late 1880s, but he was getting fed up with the workers' behavior. He didn't feel they deserved much in the way of protection by law and didn't support increases in pay or better work conditions. After his dismissal, Wilhelm and the Reichstag passed the Workers Protection Acts. This legislature protected children and women in terms of labor and also promoted better work relations between the workers and the organizations they worked for.

After Bismarck's resignation, there were a couple of different replacements before Wilhelm was satisfied with the chancellor position choice. The first to take over was Leo von Caprivi. He held the office for four years but was then replaced by Chlodwig, prince of Hohenlohe-Schillingsfürst. The prince stayed in the office for six years. In 1900, Wilhelm selected the man he said was to be his own Bismarck, Bernhard von Bülow.

Under Bismarck's foreign policy measures, Germany, France, and Russia remained in a balanced state of peace. It wasn't the most solid peace, but it was somewhat stable even if it was fragile. When news got out about Bismarck's dismissal, Russia immediately expected a change in the policy. The peaceful state started to unravel little by little as Russia and France became more involved with each other, isolating Germany bit by bit. By 1914, Germany was cast out of its once fragile alliances with Russia and France.

When Wilhelm assigned each of the chancellor selections he had made, he was laying out "The New Course," as it is referred to now in history. The office of chancellor had always been one of a respectable statesman who did his job with his own authority and power; Wilhelm, however, didn't allow for that. His chancellors were nothing more than high-level civil servants who did the work of his personal beckoning. They didn't have their own decision-making powers or roll out their own policies. Everything they did was for the betterment of Wilhelm's personal goals and was meant to further his desired achievements.

Chapter Four

Wilhelm's Diplomatic Blunders

"Whoever tries to interfere with my task I shall crush."

—Kaiser Wilhelm II

Once the chancellor situation was under control, Wilhelm turned his attention to his vision for making Germany a strong world power. In the early 1900s, he started to work on his plans for building a large German navy. He felt that a powerful and humongous naval fleet would solidify Germany as a serious superpower. He became almost obsessed with this idea about a navy. He drew picture after picture of navy ships he envisioned, even drawing the details of the vessels. He spent his time doing his drawings and making sure that all of Europe knew of his plans so that they would be leery of Germany and show him respect. All the while, he had tasked his two chancellors to take care of the domestic affairs that needed looking after. Bülow and Bethmann Hollweg, who had shown Wilhelm much loyalty, were trusted by him to do his bidding while he struck fear into the rest of the world over his foreign policy.

Wilhelm did have other passions outside of making Germany a feared world power and extending its borders for a larger place in the sun; the Kaiser was a huge supporter of the arts and sciences. He was a proponent for public education and worked to reform secondary education so that it wasn't just for the elite and certain groups of people. He also started the Kaiser Wilhelm Society to help boost scientific research. The Prussian Academy of Sciences was pressured to start new curriculums in engineering by Wilhelm's government. The Kaiser even went as far as giving the Academy of gift to fund an engineering fellowship. He worked to protect the Order of Saint John as a hereditary duty and remained as protector of the Order even after he abdicated the throne in 1918.

During the years of Wilhelm's reign, Germany suffered in its foreign affairs because of the personality of its ruler. He wasn't a very patient man, and he acted out of contempt and emotion much of the time. An impulsive and hot-tempered man, he didn't like to be challenged in his thinking, so when someone went against his views, the Kaiser would not hesitate to show his disgust.

There were specific incidents that worked to alienate Kaiser Wilhelm simply because he didn't think of how his actions would affect those around him. One famous example of this was the Kruger telegram. In 1896, Wilhelm sent a message to President Paul Kruger of the Transvaal Republic. The message was a congratulation for suppressing the British Jameson Raid. Understandably, the people of Britain were not happy at all with the news of this telegram. Wilhelm gained in disdain from the British public and lost in respect. He previously had enjoyed some support from the British and was seen in a good light with much of the English for the first 12 years he spent on the throne. In the late 1890s, however, England's public opinion started to change in regards to the Kaiser. Even those in the royal family who were related to Wilhelm didn't like him, and most of them never showed him any acceptance. British public opinion of Wilhelm would continue to decline during the course of his reign.

In regards to countries outside of Europe, Wilhelm tried to get the people of the Western world to fear Asia and to see the danger he perceived from Europe's eastern neighbors. He attempted to scare the other European leaders by speaking of the yellow peril and pointing out the triumph of Japan in the Russo-Japanese War. The yellow peril was a derogatory phrase he used to reference the wrath of the Asians, making the color of their skin central to the idea. Wilhelm also said that Japan would partner with China to fight against the West, but not many paid the Kaiser much mind.

During this time, Germany had colonies in the Pacific area and in Africa; Wilhelm tried to strengthen these during his reign, investing time and money for that purpose. Not many of the colonies thrived or became profitable though. In what is now Namibia in South West Africa, the people rose up against their German rule. The Herero and Namaqua genocide, the first genocide of the twentieth century, was born out of that revolt. Wilhelm did eventually put a stop to the genocide, but only after thousands of the local population had been killed or imprisoned in concentration camps.

Every once in a while, Wilhelm would do something diplomatically positive. One time was when he showed his support for Archduke Franz Ferdinand of Austria—the same archduke whose assassination would later be the spark that instigated World War I—when he sought to marry Sophie Chotek. Emperor Franz Joseph I of Austria was against the marriage, but Wilhelm supported the couple in their wedding plans. The wedding was eventually held in 1900.

Back in 1889, Kaiser Wilhelm visited Istanbul for the first time. The Ottoman Empire was an important stronghold of the time, and Wilhelm made several trips to the region to maintain a good relationship with the Turkish leaders. During his first visit, he managed to strike a deal to sell German rifles to the Ottoman army. In a later trip, Wilhelm went back to the Empire, this time as a guest to see Sultan Abdülhamid II.

In 1898, the Kaiser embarked on the journey to the Ottoman Eyalets, traveling by yacht to Haifa. He visited Bethlehem and Jerusalem, he went to Jaffa, and then continued to Beirut. Then he rode a train going through Aley and Zahlé, finally ending up in Damascus. The whole trip was just under a month. In Damascus, Wilhelm made a legendary speech in which he thanked everyone for their kindness and generosity. He told the Sultan and all of his followers around the world that he would always be their friend. Wilhelm made one more stop on that trip to visit

Baalbek. He then made his way back to Beirut where he would get on a ship to head back home.

During his time in the Ottoman Empire, Wilhelm cut a deal for German businesses to build the Istanbul-Baghdad railway. He also memorialized his trip by having the German Fountain built in Istanbul right across from the Mausoleum of Sultan Ahmed I. The commemorative fountain, which was gazebo-like in its style, was built in Germany and then sent in pieces to Turkey. In 1900, the fountain was assembled in Istanbul at the site it still stands today. Wilhelm would eventually have one more visit to the Ottoman Empire, but it wouldn't be until much later in 1917.

In 1900, the same year as the German Fountain was assembled, an uprising started in China. There was an anti-western, anti-colonial movement starting that turned into the Boxer Rebellion. An international combination of troops from several countries would go to China and fight to suppress the rebellion. The countries were Germany, France, Japan, Russia, Italy, America, and England.

Wilhelm didn't earn any respect for Germany in this incident, however, because his troops didn't arrive until after Japan and England's troops had already taken Peking. Peking had been where the worst battles were taking place, and Germany's reputation took a hit by their late entrance. It took another blow when Wilhelm delivered a speech to bid farewell to the troops before leaving for battle. He spoke in his very arrogant way and made it clear about his ideals of German imperial power. Wilhelm incited his troops to "in the spirit of the Huns, be merciless in battle." That speech was only issued to the public with edits. The Foreign Office took out a piece of the speech that they found to be inappropriate and on a diplomatic front, shameful and embarrassing.

Wilhelm had a somewhat narrow-minded view when it came to diplomacy. He thought a lot about Germany and its place in the sun and not enough about how his foreign affairs and diplomatic moves worked against what he was trying to attain for Germany. So, there are quite a few of what you could call blunders of diplomacy in the history of Kaiser Wilhelm II.

One of his blunders of diplomacy came to ignite a fire that turned into the Moroccan Crisis in 1905. Wilhelm visited Tangier, Morocco. While he was there he met with some representatives of Sultan Abdelaziz of Morocco. He said he was showing his support for the Sultan and his sovereignty. At the time, France had a large presence in Morocco and thus a large influence there. Wilhelm's statement about his support for the sovereignty of the Sultan was really to pose a threat to France's hold over Morocco. The Kaiser traveled all around the city, riding on a white horse and declaring his support for the Sultan. The Sultan took the bait and refused proposals from France on some changes they were suggesting for the country's government. Instead, the Sultan set up a conference in which he sought advice from other world leaders for what changes would be wise to make for his government reform. France, then, saw Wilhelm's whole visit to Morocco as a threat against their presence there as the Kaiser spoke openly about his support for Morocco's independence. The French were not happy with what looked like the Kaiser trying to open the door in Morocco for Germany to take over with influence in the country. Wilhelm was isolating Germany even more in Europe by creating conflict with its European neighbors.

The Algeciras Conference in 1906 was born out of the Moroccan Crisis that had sparked because of Germany and France's opposing sides with regards to influence in Morocco. The conference, named after the Spanish city in which it was held, went on for about three months. Wilhelm insisted that he wasn't trying to shrink France's interests at all in Morocco, he was simply trying to increase Germany's international footprint. Unfortunately for the Kaiser, this attempt to expand Germany's reach failed horribly. What he did end up doing though, was to bring France and Britain closer together. The two countries had a somewhat tumultuous past that was riddled with conflict. The issues with Wilhelm and Germany helped to unite the two governments and strengthened their agreement in the Entente Cordiale by bonding over their shared distrust of Germany's government.

In 1908, another of Wilhelm's blunders would appear in the world. This one not only upset people in other countries but had a huge impact on the people of Germany as well. Wilhelm was asked to interview for a British newspaper called the *Daily Telegraph*. He agreed to do the interview because he thought it was a great opportunity to get his ideas out to the public about Anglo-German friendship. Kaiser Wilhelm wanted to show the world that Germany could be diplomatic. But, what he ended up doing was angering some of the largest powers in the world—England, Russia, Japan, and France—because he couldn't keep his emotions in check. Wilhelm was always fiery and prone to outbursts of emotions, and this interview incited him to lose control of himself to a degree that caused his own people to call for his abdication.

During the course of the interview, Wilhelm made implications that Germany didn't have any care for Britain and its interests. He made references that Russia and France had tried to pull Germany into the middle of the Second Boer War. He also made it look like his work on building up the German navy was with the intention of using it against Japan rather than Britain. He also insulted the British people several times throughout the interview. Nothing good came out of that publication—not for Germany and not for Wilhelm. His people were embarrassed and appalled, demanding that he abdicate the throne.

After the newspaper published his interview, causing the so-called *Daily Telegraph* crisis, Wilhelm stayed out of the public eye for a few months. When he finally did come out of his low-lying state, the Kaiser forced Prince Bülow, his loyal chancellor, to resign. Wilhelm blamed him for allowing the publication to print the interview without having the text edited to a version that would be better suited for the public to see. This was one of Wilhelm's worst blunders of his career. He lost most of the respect and influence he had left for dealing with anything in the political realm. Prior to the *Daily Telegraph* crisis, Wilhelm had carried himself with a lot of self-confidence. After the crisis, however, his confidence was gone, and he slipped into a severe state of depression. He would never regain what he lost, and the depression would stay with him for the rest of his life.

Wilhelm's biggest project, regardless of any of the other matters he put energy into, was building a large and strong German navy. When he was young he had developed an interest in the British Royal Navy and as he got older that interest turned into a drive to have one of the strongest naval forces in the world. Wilhelm had felt deflated at the sight of the less than impressive German fleet at his grandmother's Diamond Jubilee celebration. He took that frustration, as well as his disappointment over failing to gain influence in South Africa, and used it to drive him in building a naval fleet that he could be proud of. Alfred von Tirpitz became Wilhelm's appointed Imperial Naval Office head in 1897 and would be instrumental in the creation of the German navy.

Tirpitz rolled out a plan that would be recognized as the Tirpitz Plan. Under the Tirpitz Plan, a fleet of German naval ships would be located in the North Sea, threatening action if Britain did not cooperate with Germany on any of their international demands. Over the course of three years, from 1897 to 1900, Wilhelm and Tirpitz did manage to build a pretty impressive naval fleet together. The two poured a lot of money into this pet project.

By 1906, Wilhelm had turned his attention and much of his finances to building bigger and better battleships, the type that was like the British Royal Navy's dreadnought. These boats were much more expensive than what the German navy had previously focused on, but Wilhelm was trying to rival the British navy, so it was necessary to have these types of battleships. But by 1914, Wilhelm had gotten his empire into serious financial trouble with his efforts to bolster the German navy.

Chapter Five

Leading Germany to World War I

"Ruthlessness and weakness will start the most terrifying war of the world; whose purpose is to destroy Germany."

—Kaiser Wilhelm II

For years Wilhelm had been alienating Germany further and further from countries Bismarck had previously worked very hard to keep good relations with. Tensions in Europe were rising throughout the course of his reign. Something terrible was brewing, and Wilhelm was very much a part of what was stirring the pot leading up to World War I.

The Archduke Franz Ferdinand of Austria was a good friend of Wilhelm's. On June 28, 1914, Ferdinand was assassinated. Wilhelm was saddened and completely taken aback. The assassination had been carried out in Sarajevo by a Serbian underground group known as the Black Hand. In response to the killing, Wilhelm extended his support to Austria-Hungary to take down the Black Hand. He also showed that any amount of force that Austria needed to use against Serbia was not only appropriate but needed as they were the power behind the movement that led to the assassination of Wilhelm's friend. This sanctioning of the use of force by the Kaiser is known as "the blank cheque."

Wilhelm normally took a yearly trip to cruise the North Sea, but with the issues in Austria-Hungary and the looming conflict with Serbia, he didn't want to go in 1914. Only at the urging from his courtiers did he decide to make the trip. He was gone on his travels when Serbia received their threatening ultimatum from Austria-Hungary. Wilhelm made a fast return to Germany. When he arrived, he wrote about what a "brilliant solution" there had been between Austria-Hungary and Serbia. He was praising them all for coming to an agreement that didn't include war.

But what Wilhelm didn't know was that Franz Joseph I of Austria had already been convinced by his ministers and generals to declare war on Serbia. He had already signed on the dotted line. This made Russia start to make their move against Austria. The Russian troops were mobilized to protect Serbia. News of this mobilization came to Wilhelm on July 30, 1914. He was informed that Russia would not cease their movement under any conditions.

Wilhelm knew that this meant that war was coming to Germany because of Germany's treaties with Austria. But Wilhelm was certain that it wouldn't just be Russia knocking on the door; he said that he knew this meant that "England, Russia and France have agreed among themselves" that it was time to take out Germany and wage an all-out war against them. Wilhelm was starting to panic. His beloved German Empire was about to have to battle it out on two fronts and all after he'd virtually bankrupted the country. He knew that England would take part in the war if he attacked France by way of Belgium, who was neutral. And Russia was already mobilized against Austria from the east.

There had been a plan back in 1905 for the initialization of troops for a one-front war with the French Republic. The plan had been created by General von Schlieffen. In 1914, the general's nephew, Helmuth von Moltke, chose the Schlieffen plan as one that could be adapted for a two-front war by Germany. But when Wilhelm asked younger Moltke about trying to redirect the primary attack to go against Russia, Moltke responded that it would be impossible. Wilhelm didn't like the answer he received. He insulted the young Moltke by saying, "Your uncle would have given me a different answer!"

In the adaptation of the Schlieffen plan for the war on two fronts, the idea was that Germany would attack the weaker country first. That country was France. Then it would go on to attack Russia after that. The problem with the plan, however, was that the German leaders were all thinking that Russia wouldn't be prepared for a war. They were wrong; the Russians had already mobilized their military in defense of Serbia.

While Kaiser Wilhelm had played such a huge role in creating the friction between the countries involved in World War I, his role as a leader of the Germans who were fighting the war became smaller and smaller. His power dwindled as the years of the war went on. The Schlieffen plan didn't work, failing miserably. Two years into the war, the German Empire was basically being run by its military officials; Field Marshal Paul von Hindenburg and General Erich Ludendorff were leading their country through the war. Meanwhile, Wilhelm was performing award ceremonies and minor projects of honorable duties. The Kaiser fell more and more into his non-reality. He was no longer a part of any decision making. There were times when he was very much of a defeated state of mind and other times when he flew high on the thoughts of a complete victory over the other European powers. His back and forth usually ebbed and flowed with what was happening on the war fronts.

Even though he was not making decisions in the war, Wilhelm was the German emperor. That meant that he still had the ultimate say as to who would be appointed to certain political positions. Ludendorff and Hindenburg wanted Wilhelm to find a replacement for Bethmann-Hollweg as chancellor in 1917. Wilhelm asked them who they would like to see appointed. Ludendorff made a suggestion of Georg Michaelis. Even though he didn't know anything about Michaelis, Wilhelm agreed to appoint him as chancellor at his military leader's request.

In the fall of 1918, things really spiraled all the way down for Wilhelm. President Woodrow Wilson of the United States announced that the German Kaiser would not be permitted to take place in any negotiations of peace. As a result of that announcement, Wilhelm lost what little bit of good public opinion that he had left as well as the backing of his civilian government officials. He also lost all respect from the German army. There was nothing left for Kaiser Wilhelm to do as a leader of the German Empire. His days as the leader of Germany and Prussia were coming to an end, along with the end of the war.

Chapter Six

The Last German Emperor

"I herewith renounce for all time claims to the throne of Prussia and to the German Imperial throne connected therewith."

—Kaiser Wilhelm II

At about the time of the end of the First World War, a mutiny started in Berlin. The German Revolution broke out; the German people wanted nothing more to do with Wilhelm. All support of the Kaiser was gone, and the public was crying out for his abdication of the throne.

Wilhelm, even with all that was happening and with having no support from the people, was having a hard time deciding if he should abdicate his position. Part of his problem was that he thought he could keep one of the seats he occupied, even if he gave up the other. Wilhelm did not understand that he wasn't in a position of deciding on one crown over the other. The written constitution stated that the two crowns were always to be tied together. Only one individual would hold the positions of German emperor and Prussian king; if Wilhelm decided to abdicate one throne, he would be choosing to abdicate the other as well.

Wilhelm learned of the constitutional laws surrounding the inability to retain one of his crowns when another political figure made a move to get him abdicated. Chancellor Prince Max von Baden decided simply to make the announcement himself that Wilhelm was abdicating. On November 9, 1918, he told the world of Wilhelm's abdication in an attempt to save the German monarchy. The revolution was growing, and something had to be done to stop it. Max's attempt was a failure, however, and resulted in his own forced resignation later that day. Also during that day, Germany was labeled a republic by future President Friedrich Ebert's minister, Philipp Scheidemann.

On November 10, the day after Chancellor von Baden had announced the Kaiser's abdication, Wilhelm left Germany and fled to the Netherlands. The country had stayed neutral during the time of the war, making it a good place to go into exile.

The last straw for Wilhelm was when Paul von Hindenburg, someone who had shown the Kaiser much support over the years, told him to abdicate his position as the leader of the German people and Prussia. The military officials had told Wilhelm that although the army would come home in an orderly fashion and would behave properly under Hindenburg's control, they would not be showing any support or fight for the Kaiser. No one would support Wilhelm as the German emperor anymore. He finally accepted his reality and released his official statement of abdication from the two thrones on

November 28, 1918. The Hohenzollerns had reigned in Prussia for 400 years, but now their rule was over.

The funny thing in all of this is that Otto von Bismarck, whom Wilhelm had forced to resign early on in his reign, had warned the Kaiser about the militarists' influence. During their last meeting at Bismarck's estate, he had said to Wilhelm, "Your Majesty, so long as you have this present officer corps, you can do as you please. But when this is no longer the case, it will be very different for you." Bismarck also predicted that in 20 years' time, things would fall apart for Wilhelm and the German Empire under his rule. His very words were, "the crash will come 20 years after my departure if things go on like this." He was right.

On June 28, 1919, the Treaty of Versailles was signed, officially ending the state of war between Germany and the Allied Powers. In Article 227 of the treaty, the reasons behind Kaiser Wilhelm's prosecution were listed. He was to be prosecuted "for a supreme offense against international morality and the sanctity of treaties." But luckily for Wilhelm, the government of the Netherlands would not agree to extradite him. While many of the Allies were calling for the extradition, United States President Wilson was one who actually didn't support the idea. He wanted Wilhelm to be left where he was, exiled to the Netherlands. Unlike what Wilhelm ever did during his reign, President Wilson was thinking of the state of affairs in the global world. He thought that extraditing the fallen Kaiser would only weaken the international bonds that were being forged, and peace would be lost.

So, Wilhelm was allowed to stay in the Netherlands. Eventually, he bought himself a house out in the country. The house, called Huis Doorn, was located in the municipality of Doorn. He moved there on May 15, 1920, and lived out the rest of his life in that home. Wilhelm wasn't without his possessions, as it may be thought since he was living in exile; the newly named Weimar Republic did let Wilhelm retrieve many of his belongings from the New Palace at Potsdam. He even got to keep a car and a boat.

Chapter Seven

Wilhelm's Exile and World War II

"For the first time, I am ashamed to be a German."

—Kaiser Wilhelm II

While in exile, Wilhelm tried to clear his name of any wrongdoing when it came to the cause of the Great War. In 1922, he wrote and had published a thin volume of his memoirs in which he defended the way he behaved on matters of foreign policy and also denounced the idea that he was in any way responsible for starting the international conflict.

Wilhelm became a very social person while living in the Netherlands. He learned to speak Dutch and immersed himself in the Dutch culture, often entertaining guests—some of which were of high social standing—at his house. He made sure to keep himself up to date on all the goings-on of Europe as well.

Earlier in life, Wilhelm had developed a passion for archaeology and had done some excavation at the Temple of Artemis in Corfu. In exile, he cultivated that passion, spending a lot of time learning about his archaeological interest. He also spent time hunting and had hunted thousands of animals by the end of his 20 years in exile. One other somewhat strange pastime he took up in the Netherlands was chopping wood. He chopped down thousands of trees over two decades living in Huis Doorn.

While Wilhelm was not a Nazi, he did get excited when early on in the 1930s the German Nazi Party had some great triumphs. His hope was that there would be renewed interest from the German people and their government in bringing back the monarchy. His thinking was that maybe his oldest grandson could become the next Kaiser. Wilhelm had remarried while in exile, and his wife, Hermine, sent a request petitioning for the appointment of Wilhelm's grandson as a new Kaiser. Adolf Hitler, however, would hear nothing of the idea. He had fought in the war and was disgusted with Wilhelm and what he had done to the German Empire. He blamed Wilhelm for what he saw as the country's biggest failure and ignored the request of Wilhelm's wife on behalf of her husband.

Over time, Wilhelm began to distrust Hitler. He was hearing rumors about Hitler's treatment of people who were part of the Nazi party, and he even heard that Hitler had one of the chancellors' wives murdered. In response to the news, Wilhelm said, "We have ceased to live under the rule of law and everyone must be prepared for the possibility that the Nazis will push their way in and put them up against the wall!"

Wilhelm grew to dislike Hitler for what he was doing to Germany, stating that Hitler was creating gangsters out of his military. Wilhelm also said that while Hitler may be able to win at things, there would be no glory in those wins because of the way he was conducting business. Wilhelm thought Hitler to be impressive in his ability to build legions of his militants, but he strongly believed that he could not build a nation that way. He said that Hitler didn't acknowledge what a nation was all about—family, religion, and traditions. That's what countries were built on according to Wilhelm, not on military alone.

At the end of 1938, Wilhelm said in reference to his thoughts on Hitler's version of Germany, "For a few months I was inclined to believe in National Socialism. I thought of it as a necessary fever. And I was gratified to see that there were, associated with it for a time, some of the wisest and most outstanding Germans. But these, one by one, he has got rid of or even killed . . . He has left nothing but a bunch of shirted gangsters! This man could bring home victories to our people each year, without bringing them either glory or danger. But of our Germany, which was a nation of poets and musicians, of artists and soldiers, he has made a nation of hysterics and hermits, engulfed in a mob and led by a thousand liars or fanatics."

Later though, Wilhelm would congratulate Hitler on the success he had at the beginning of World War II, claiming he only wanted to rile Hitler with his antics. Wilhelm was just trying to amuse himself and get under Hitler's skin. After the Netherlands surrendered, Wilhelm sent, "My Fuhrer, I congratulate you and hope that under your marvelous leadership the German monarchy will be restored completely." Hitler found the telegram to be obnoxious and referred to Wilhelm as an idiot. Another telegram was sent after Paris had fallen. It said simply, "Congratulations, you have won using my troops." Ever the instigator, Wilhelm was certainly staying true to himself.

In 1940, the Nazis invaded the Netherlands. Wilhelm was pretty much in retirement by then and had drawn himself back from the public eye. He was given the option of finding asylum in England with the invasion taking place, but Wilhelm refused to leave his home at Doorn. He said he would just rather die there in his house. While the old Kaiser didn't die due to the invasion, he would have his wish in the end.

Chapter Eight

Late Life and Death

"I see myself as an instrument of the Almighty and go on my way, regardless of transient opinions and views."

—Kaiser Wilhelm II

Wilhelm spent his whole life, in essence, trying to secure Germany's place in the world. He believed so strongly in Germany that even after being exiled and losing the support of his people, he still wanted good things for his country. Wilhelm equated his monarchy with being of Christ and England of being of Satan. Of the English people, he said they were "Freemasons thoroughly infected by Juda." He was adamant that the British needed to be liberated from the hold that Juda had on them. Wilhelm had defended himself and accepted no blame for the start of the First World War in 1914; instead, he blamed the war and the Second World War on the Freemasons and Jews. He held the belief that the two groups were trying to dominate the world and that they would do it with English and American money.

Wilhelm held on to the idea of Germany as a leading world power until the end of his life. In a letter to his sister shortly before his death, Wilhelm referred to what he said was going to end up being the United States of

Europe—a European continent of unity which would be ruled by Germany.

In 1941, Wilhelm's house was being guarded by a troop of German soldiers on orders by one of the generals. Wilhelm was 82 years old at the time. When Hitler found out that the general had ordered the soldiers to provide guardianship to Wilhelm at Huis Doorn, he was infuriated and fired the general immediately.

On June 4, 1941, Wilhelm II died of a pulmonary embolus at his home in Doorn. While Hitler wasn't fond of Wilhelm, he saw a political opportunity in his death and wanted to bring Wilhelm's body back to Berlin to have a proper state funeral in his homeland. Hitler thought Wilhelm to be symbolic of Germany and its people and representative of the Germans who fought in the war. His thought was also that this would show the people of Germany that the Third Reich was directly descended from the German Empire of old; it would be a way to gain support from the people who had not already recognized the Nazi way as the right way.

But in the end, Wilhelm's body never returned to Germany. He had made his wishes clear in life that he would not go back to Germany until the German monarchy was fully restored. Those wishes were acknowledged and upheld by the Dutch government. Wilhelm's body would never return to Germany because the monarchy was never again restored. He was given a military funeral in the Netherlands. Some of Wilhelm's other requests were ignored, however. He hadn't wanted any Nazi symbolism or icons to be displayed at his funeral, but there are photographs showing that this wish was not respected.

Huis Doorn was the last place that Wilhelm ever lived, and he is still there today. His remains are in a mausoleum on the Huis Doorn property. There are still people who visit his last home, and to some he is a very important character in the history of their heritage as he was the last German emperor ever to reign.

Conclusion

Kaiser Wilhelm II may not have gone down in history as the most successful ruler of Germany, but he certainly went down in history as one of the most famous. The world changed a great deal under his control. Even having been born of parents from two different royal lines, Wilhelm couldn't find a way to unite the continent using his heritage. In fact, he did quite the opposite.

Wilhelm was a boisterous and often impulsive man. He would lash out at those who opposed him and his beliefs. While he was very intelligent, his inability to think outside of what he saw as the right and entitled path for Germany ultimately led to his abdication and exile out of his country.

It's hard to say how different history might look if Wilhelm had never been in power. His take on foreign policy was not one that promoted peace and stability. He claimed to be guilt free in terms of the start of World War I, but many historians do put the blame squarely on the German Kaiser. It's safe to say that he had a hand in what led to the outbreak of war in some shape or form.

After his reign as German emperor and Prussian king, Wilhelm lived the last quarter of his life in exile in the Netherlands. Even from his little corner of the world where he had no great power as he had before, Wilhelm still fought in his own way for Germany. He wanted the monarchy restored all the way to his dying day. He wanted to see his family continue to rule the country he so loved and supported. But it would never come to be. With the end of Wilhelm's reign came the end of an era. The world would never again know another German emperor.